PARISH REGIST

C000112062

Introduction

Parish registers are the major source of basic genealogical information from the time they were instituted, in 1538, to the start of
national registration in July 1837. Not all of them did start in
1538, and not all that started then, or within twenty years of that
date, now survive. Fires, damp, carelessness, loss, vandalism and
simple theft have taken their toll over the years. Some were infin-
itely better kept than others, are more legible, more complete, more
detailed. It depended entirely on the clergyman or clerk how useful
the register entries are, with no rules at all (except for a brief
period in the seventeenth century) until 1754, when the first printed
forms for marriages were introduced, and until 1813 for baptisms and
burials. Some parish registers have gaps which make it difficult to
trace a pedigree back, some have illuminating comments which make the
family historian's task easier.

Even the most copper-bottomed nonconformist family will find the majority of their story in the church registers, especially before 1780. Atheism was rare, and failure to attend church was kept in check by penalties and economic pressures until the last century when a gradual process of social emancipation began. Present day church attenders go because they are committed Christians.

Most parish registers of any age are no longer kept in the parish churches, but in central Record Offices, which have storage and security facilities not available in a church. In England, the county or a metropolitan borough is the normal administrator of such an office. In Wales, many registers were collected at the National Library, at Aberystwyth, and County Record Offices have only been established in recent years. In Scotland, all old registers were called in to Edinburgh, where they may be seen. The same thing happened in Ireland, but the Office in Dublin was burnt, and many of the parish registers with it, which adds problems to Irish research.

There are also numerous copies, contemporary 'transcripts' or modern printed or typed ones, which may ease your task. Indexes, computerised and otherwise, may shorten the search, but, in the end, you will need to spend some time just systematically searching through the parish registers. This Guide explains what you will find there, and what some of the forms and comments mean.

Can we use parish registers instead of certificates?

In theory, everyone's births, marriages and deaths from 1837 (for England and Wales) are recorded at the General Register Office (at St. Catherine's House, 10 Kingsway, London WC2B 6JP). But those certificates cost £5.00 each, so why can't we use parish registers instead? After all, everyone used to go to church in the old days. In fact, neither proposition is true.

Most people in 1837 probably did attend some form of religious worship, at least off and on. In villages, this is more correct than in towns, where family pressures and church-associated charity were less common. But church attendance fell off slowly during the century, and sharply in the present century, and in most places a variety of chapels competed very successfully for the faithful. Town populations multiplied enormously, and new parishes were created to accommodate the expected large congregations, so that in London and the great industrial cities, you will be faced with a choice of several sets of registers, even if you know for sure that your ancestors were Anglicans. The last century was a time of great mobility, so that a long search in one place may throw up one baptism – before they move to the next parish or town. If you discover from the censuses that your ancestors were born in a named rural area, that is a far better bet, but even then, your lot may be conspicuous by their absence from the church registers, because they were the only Bible Christians in the district and walked twenty miles every Sunday to worship. Chapel registers are by no means as easy to come by, after 1837, in general.

Assuming that your family were good Church of England folk, and stayed in one place, will the registers give you all you need? Possibly not, since the amount of detail is not the same as in certificates.

Marriage registers after 1st July 1837 do give exactly the same information. There are two entries to a page, identical in form with certificates. They will tell you the *names of groom and bride*; the *ages*, exact or 'full', meaning 21 or more; the *marital status*; the *occupation*, of the groom at least; the *place of residence*, which may be just 'of this parish'; the *name and occupation of the two fathers*. You also get the actual signatures (or marks) of the couple and their witnesses. However, you cannot legally photocopy the entries for less than £5, as agreed by the Registrar General. Most Record Offices will permit a photograph, however.

The snag is that marriages do not necessarily take place where the couple later lived. It was common to marry in the bride's home parish, or where she was working at the time. You could search for years for a Hampshire couple who happened to marry in London or Gloucester. National registration gets over this problem with a consolidated index for the whole of England and Wales from 1837 (with a similar Scottish index from 1855 and an Irish (Protestant) one from 1845).

Baptism and Burial registers show less detail than the equivalent certificates of birth and death. You can judge if this matters.

Baptismal entries probably will not show the date of birth, and baptism may be much delayed. They also very rarely indeed show the maiden name of the mother. You may have it from other sources, but things can get confusing if there are two John and Mary Smiths, or if one man marries two wives of the same name in succession. Carefully cross-checking with burial registers and censuses is necessary.

However, some births in the earlier years of registration (and even later in cities) were never officially notified, so that the census and baptismal entries are the only evidence of existence. Parish register entries are accepted as proof of age for pensions purposes therefore, and parents who left it late lose their offspring money. The unbaptised have to rely on tracing midwives in their nineties, or finding certain other documentary evidence.

Burial registers do not give the precise date of death, the marital status, occupation, cause of death, or the name of the informant (a probable relative). They do give *ages* - not necessarily accurate, nor the same as the certificate age. As a bonus, they may state the normal address or parish of someone who happens to die while visiting a daughter - which a certificate in England would not. If the death was violent or sudden, the register should note 'by coroner's order' which will alert you to look for an inquest report in the local paper.

Unless you come from a family of zealous churchgoers, the value of parish registers to you will diminish as the century wears on. Searching a city parish, or several of them, is a very time-consuming business. A combination of certificates and censuses can take you more rapidly back to 1837, and it is before this that the parish registers may become your prime source.

Parish registers from 1813

Rose's Act of 1812 established for the first time a printed format for baptism and burial registers and amended marriage registers slightly. The *Baptismal registers* provided columns for the *date of baptism*, the *surname* and *Christian name of the child and its parents*, the *occupation of the father* and their *residence*. In the country this was probably just the village or hamlet name, or possibly a farm, though in towns a street address is normally given. The final column gives the signature of the clergyman. Sometimes, conscientious clergy squeeze a date of birth into the margin. There are eight entries to a page.

In the case of illegitimate children, the mother's Christian and surname is stated (and, occasionally, the father's full name too) with the addition of 'base born' and her occupation, or 'spinster', 'single', in the penultimate column. Alternatively, the child may be given the father's full name as forenames, 'John Smith Jones, base-born of Mary Jones', with the hope that they would later marry and the second surname could be dropped. Double forenames were then rare, except in the gentry and upper middle classes, outside London and Yorkshire (see also under 'Illegitimacy', page 15).

Burial registers have similar columns, with space for the *date*, *Christian* and *surname*, *age* and *residence* of the deceased, but not, unfortunately, the occupation or any other comment, which had sometimes been added to burial entries in plain-paged registers. Just occasionally, nevertheless, remarks are added - regularly if the burial is 'by coroner's warrant', possibly if the death was in odd circumstances or that of a gentleman, cleric or parish clerk. The 'name of officiating clergyman' is rarely important, though worth noting if it is not the usual one - he may be a relative.

This type of baptism and burial register continued after 1837, until modern times. The marriage registers, however, changed completely in 1837, to the 'certificate' form.

There had been printed *Marriage registers* since 1754, and Rose's Act merely changed the number of entries per page from four to three. There were blank spaces on the pages in which the clerk or clergyman had to write the *names* and *parishes* of the parties, and the *date*. There was room to include the *marital status* of both, but this is sometimes omitted. There was a space to show if the marriage was by *licence* or *banns*, and, if one or both was *under 21*, a *'minor'*, then room to write 'with consent of father/parents'. Some clergy got confused and entered 'with consent of friends' for the marriages of adults who needed no such agreement. The couple then had to sign, or make a mark to their names. Occasionally, the signature does not tally completely with the spelling of the name written above. The clergyman himself then signed, and two or more *witnesses*. These tended to be relatives (contemporaries rather than parents), though lonely folk might call in people who lived near the church. Look out for a very regular signature, which may be that of the parish clerk.

BAPTISMS solemnized in the Parish of *Handborough.* in the County of *Oxon* in the Year 18*27*

| When Baptized. | Child's Christian Name. | Parents Name. | | Abode. | Quality, Trade, or Profession. | By whom the Ceremony was performed. |
		Christian.	Surname.			
1827. June 3 No. 425.	June 3 Susan daughter of	William and Elizabeth		Buckingham — Handbro.	Labourer	Thos Spindle Curate
June 3. No. 426.	Amelia daughter of	James & Mary	Long	Handbro	Tradesman	Wm Spindle Curate.
July 15th No. 427.	Anne Mary illegitimate daughter of	Dinah	Leach	Handbro.		Thos Spindle Curate.

Nineteenth century registers

Entries of Baptisms and Burials at Han(d)borough, Oxfordshire, in the standard printed form books introduced by Rose's Act from 1813.

BURIALS in the Parish of *Handborough* in the County of *Oxford* in the Year 18*47*

Name.	Abode.	When buried.	Age.	By whom the Ceremony was performed.
Sarah Slatter No. 649.	Long Handbro'	July 2	49	T. Robinson
Rosetta Woodward No. 650.	Witney, Union Workhouse	July 20	5 mths	Frank B. Wright, Curate

5

Before 1837, everyone (except Jews and Quakers) had to be married in church, even if they were Strict Baptists or 'Independents'. From July 1837, chapel members could wed in their own chapel, if it was licensed for the purpose, which may not have happened till 1890. Civil marriage before the Registrar was possible from July 1837, though many continued to use the parish church for weddings only. By 1900, about ten per cent of couples were married in a Registry Office.

Marriage Registers from 1754: the Hardwicke Act

In theory, marriages were always supposed to have taken place in the parish church, if by banns, though those who could afford licences could marry elsewhere, normally in a nominated church. However, there was nothing to prevent any person who had ever taken Holy Orders, whether or no he was a beneficed clergyman, from marrying anyone anywhere at any time. By the middle of the eighteenth century, this had led to great abuses, and various runaway marriages of heiresses had made this a problem to the legislating classes.   Philip Yorke, Lord Hardwicke, therefore introduced in 1753 the Act which bears his name, whose purpose was 'the better prevention of clandestine marriages'.

From March 1754, marriages were only legal if they took place after banns in the parish church of one of the parties, often that of the bride, normally by the parish clergyman, though he could permit another beneficed clergyman, such as a relative of the parties, to officiate. Alternatively, marriages by licence were still permitted at churches where banns had formerly been accustomed to be published, which cut out the old 'marriage shops' (see page 17).   New churches built to cope with increased population in some areas had to be specifically licensed before legal marriages could take place.

Registers in compliance with the Act are generally about 18" tall, often covered in brown suede, and each page contains four printed forms with spaces to insert the variable details. The *name* of bride and groom, the *parish* of both and quite frequently the *marital status* and sometimes the man's *occupation* could be entered; also the *date* of the ceremony, and whether it was by *banns* or *licence*. The *signatures* of the couple, the clergyman and two or more *witnesses* were also demanded, for the first time. If they could not write, they made marks to their names written by the clerk.

Because the number of entries per page was standard, it was no longer possible to forge an extra one or cut out an entry without its showing. Even when this was done, the entry could be traced in the copy sent to the Bishop each year (see page 23). Most of the clergy numbered each entry as well, for even greater security. The witnesses who signed could be called to vouch for the accuracy of the record too.

It should be borne in mind that 'of this parish' does not necessarily imply long residence there. Three weeks was the legal requirement, though the more conscientious clergy would describe such an incomer as 'sojourner here', and, rarely, even note his actual parish of settlement. Sometimes the motive for moving into a parish before the marriage was to avoid two sets of banns fees, and the trouble of collecting a certificate (that they had been called) from the distant parish.

The main purpose of the Act had been to prevent runaway marriages of heiresses and consequent loss of control of their fortunes. Minors needed the consent of their parent to contract a valid marriage anyway and even with slightly older heiresses, parish clergy were vulnerable to pressure if they allowed such a marriage. Preferment was in the hands of gentry fathers and guardians, so the younger or ambitious clergy stuck to the letter of the law. The outlook for the adventurer, or even the honest but poor lover, was not so good. However, the Hardwicke Act did not apply to Scotland, and some young couples ran away there to marry. At Gretna Green and other places just over the border, the system was well established, since it was not even necessary to find a priest or call banns. A declaration of intent before two witnesses was enough. Most of these runaway marriages, once the damage was done, were re-solemnised in England.

Banns and licences

Banns had to be called for three Sundays in open church, but formal records are rare before 1754. The 'Hardwicke' registers had printed spaces for banns, either at the beginning of the book, with actual marriages starting halfway through, or combined with the marriage entries themselves. The clerk tended to write down the names for which banns were to be called as requested, and some of these were not followed by a wedding in the parish, or at all. In this case, the 'marriage' space below may be filled in with a licence marriage, or the next banns marriage as it occurred. Banns may be stopped after one or two Sundays and the reason written in - usually one party was under age, but some changed their minds. Completed banns are not proof that a marriage took place, but a guide.

Some banns books, especially those used from 1823, are separate from marriage registers, but always worth studying. There is often a gap between 1813 and 1822, possibly because Rose Act books tended not to include banns pages. The 1824 Marriage Act ordered keeping of actual banns registers again, instead of 'loose papers'.

The banns may state a parish of origin which is not in the actual register, or be the only clue where to look for the actual wedding, in the bride's parish.

If people wanted to marry in a hurry, or without local publicity, or outside their own parishes, they obtained a licence. It was partly a status symbol, used at first by the gentry, and then by better-off farmers and tradesmen, to show they had arrived socially. It was also used by nonconformists, and for the marriages of parents of bastards. In this case, it was paid for by the parish overseers, while they had the man nailed down and more or less willing.

Licences could be obtained from the Bishop or Archdeacon, or a deputy appointed to serve a rural area (a coveted appointment of profit); clergy in 'peculiars' (parishes exempt from normal church jurisdiction); and, above these, the two Archbishops, through their officials. A 'common licence' named two parishes where the marriage could take place, one of which should have been the home parish, but it could be used elsewhere in practice, often at the nearest church to hand after obtaining it, possibly the one from which the licence was issued.

An Archbishop's licence allowed a wider range of parishes, again specified in the paper. A 'special licence' allowed marriage anywhere – these are rare except in wartime or among the highly mobile upper class.

Bishops' and Archdeacons' licences and sometimes their official surrogates' should be filed in the Diocesan registry (mostly trans-ferred to County Record Offices now) and are sometimes indexed or listed (see the FFHS Guide to *Bishops' Transcripts and Marriage Licences*, page 32). Records of licences issued by surrogates or in peculiars often have not been preserved.

Where there is a filed record, you should find an Allegation and Bond, which ought to give the ages of the parties, the name of the father if one was a minor, and the name of the bondsmen, who may be relatives.

Ages are not totally reliable. Minors might claim they were over 21 and ages may be given as '21 and upwards', '30 and upwards', which could be a long way upwards, especially for second marriages. The bond was forfeit if the information sworn was wrong or the marriage was not performed, though I have no evidence that this happened if the parties changed their minds rapidly. The actual licence was handed by the groom to the clergyman, and only rarely survives, if it happened to be tucked into a register or the parish chest.

Many gentry holders of licences obtained them so that they could marry in London, or a town convenient for their friends to gather. Their range of 'marriage horizon' tended to be wider, so that they had to allow for relatives travelling some distance. This makes pre-1754 marriages difficult to trace and emphasises the importance of marriages indexes (see pages 29-30, 32).

Quakers and Jews

Because of the difference in their ceremonies and the very much better record keeping, Quakers and Jews were exempt from the provis-ions of the Hardwicke Marriage Act. The Sephardic Jewish marriages have been published to 1837 and the Ashkenazi marriage records are held by the United Synagogue, Woburn House, Upper Woburn Place, London WC1H 0EZ for the Dukes Place Synagogue and the Western Synagogue's at Crawford Place, W1H 1JD. Non-London synagogues should be approached direct (see also *My Ancestor was Jewish*, page 32).

The Society of Friends (Quakers) operated a much stricter system than the Church of England, investigating at length those who applied to marry to make sure they were in good standing and not in any way involved with anyone else. The marriage took place before the whole

Meeting, and the registers give the name of the parties, the occupation of the husband, their residence, the name of both parents of each, and the residence of the parents - which is better than any Anglican register, even after 1837. The couple signed, then more or less all those present, starting with relatives.

All Quaker registers had to be handed in to the Registrar General in 1837 (in common with other nonconformist registers) and are now at the Public Record Office, Chancery Lane, London WC2A 1LR. However, before they were deposited, a complete Digest was made, with an alphabetical index for each Meeting area. This includes the parents' name of the person indexed, and it is necessary to check both parties for the complete family information. Witnesses' names can only be found in the original registers. Some County Record Offices hold film copies of their local nonconformist registers, including Quakers'. They cover the period from the mid-seventeenth century to 1837. Digests for the whole country may be found at Friends' House, Euston Road, London NW1 2BJ, and consulted for a modest fee. There are similar Digests and registers of births and deaths (see *My Ancestors were Quakers*, page 32).

Nonconformists and Catholics

There was no legal way for Protestant or Catholic dissenters to marry in their own faith after 1754. Catholics tended to wed secretly before their priest and then again in the parish church, especially where property was at stake. Methodists married in church without much problem, since they originally thought of themselves somewhat as a reforming sect of the Church of England. Baptists and Independents sometimes continued to 'marry' at their meeting, but this was liable to cause problems for their children. If they went to the local parish church, where they were known, the gleeful parson often tried to force baptism on them as a condition for performing marriage. Instances are recorded of the unwilling postulant making obscene gestures or turning his back at the last minute, and having quite the wrong part of his anatomy signed with the cross.

It was possible to avoid this indignity by getting a licence and going to a distant parish. There were still some which had the right to issue their own licences. Churches in large towns were much less fussy about the religious condition of their couples, and those who could afford to get to St George's, Hanover Square or St Marylebone in London, or Birmingham St Philip's or Manchester Cathedral further north, still found a 'two chairs, no waiting' attitude (see also page 16, for the laxer conditions before 1754).

The eighteenth century registers

Apart from Marriage registers after 1754, there was no set form for keeping registers. There was a legal requirement, from 1598, that the books had to be parchment, but parchment cost money. Often you will find a statement that the Reverend Mr X, or two named church-wardens, had paid so-and-so for the purchase.

Some of the smallest parishes made do with a little book of very poor quality. Large parishes may have separate books for baptisms and burials, especially in later years. Sometimes the registers record events mixed as they happened, but more usually they divide up the baptisms, marriages and burials. Often the baptisms are at the front of the book, the burials starting at the other end, by turning the book upside down, and the marriages (to 1753) in the middle. Space may have run out for the baptisms, so they were tucked in on half pages among the marriages, or started again in the 'burial' end of the book. If you are searching one of these registers, make sure you find all the years, noting if you miss some. If the registers are in a Record Office, they should catalogue exactly what is in the register, so check if there seems to be a gap. Sometimes there really is a gap, where a page has fallen out of the register long ago, or been torn out later, or where the parson left a space to copy in some of the events when he had time, and never did. There may be a bishop's transcript to cover this gap (see page 23).

It was entirely up to the clerk or clergyman what form his entry took. Usually by this stage, the full date of baptism, the name of the child and the Christian names of father and mother are given. But frequently in the north only the father's name was stated. This caused obvious problems when questions of inheritance arose, since there were endless duplications of names like 'John Thorpe' or 'Joseph Rhodes'. Perhaps to counteract this, in 1777 the Archbishop of York suggested that improvements should be made in the amount of detail in registers, and, notably in the deanery of Doncaster, this was zealously done. For a period of ten years or so, baptismal entries gave full details of the mother, her maiden name, and, for a time, included the occupation of the father, his residence, the name of his father and his wife's, and their residences, and even the child's position in the family ('fourth child and second son of'). This is a family historian's dream where it occurs.

There was a general tendency as the century wore on to add more detail to the registers, especially where a clergyman had been resident a long time and knew his parishioners well. The mother's maiden name appears in baptisms fairly often in the 1790-1812 period, not necessarily for many years at a stretch. Father's occupation may be given particularly if there are two couples named, e.g. John and Mary Harris, in the same parish. If both are labourers, one may be described by his seniority, or his residence. Occasionally, dates of birth may be included for a while. It is entirely at the whim of the clergyman concerned.

There is often extra detail in burials. Here again, entirely at the whim of the clergyman, there may be occupations, ages, locations, the name of the father of a child or the husband of a woman. There are sometimes comments on the character of the late not necessarily lamented. As many people could not read nor write, the comments are uninhibited by the laws of libel or fear of retribution. For the literate part of the congregation, the comments may be in Latin,

Chiddingly

Births & Baptisms

Names	1787.	Born	Bapt:
Guy	John, Son of Walter & Ann Guy	Dec.r 1. 86	Jan.ry 8.
Ellis	Sarah, Daur. of Henry & Lucy Ellis	Dec.r 22. 86	Jan.ry 8.
Willard	Catherine, Daur. of Jos: & Ann Willard	Nov.r 26. 86	Jan.ry 29.
Thorpe	Ann, Daur. of Wm & Ann Thorpe	Jan.ry 17.	Feb.ry 12.
Oliver	Phillis, Daur. of Thos & Eliz.th Oliver	Oct.r 9. 86	Feb.ry 11.
Willey	Keziah, Daur. of John & Mary W.y Travellers	Feb.ry 28.	March 11.

Eighteenth century registers

Above: an example of a Baptism register also giving dates of birth.
Below: the standard form of Marriage register introduced by the
Hardwicke Act from 1754. Both examples are from Chiddingly, Sussex.

No. William Barnett — — — — of this Parish
Batchelor — And Ann Healey of this parish
Spinster — — — — — — — were
Married in this Church by Banns — — — —
this Eigth — Day of June, in the Year One Thousand Seven Hundred
and Seventy Eight By me John Lewis Curate
This Marriage was solemnized between Us { The + mark of Wm Barnett
The + mark of Ann Healey
In the Presence of { S. Parry & Lawes
J. Mepenton

No. Edward Compton Widower & Mary Stockbridge Spinster of this Parish
— — — — — — — —
— — — — — — — were
Married in this Church by Licence
this 21st Day of June in the Year One Thousand Seven — Hundred
and Seventy eight — By me J. Cleoburey vic.
This Marriage was solemnized between Us { Edd Compton
Mary Stockbridge + her mark
In the Presence of { Doctor Stacey
Hannah Stacey

Greek, French or even personal shorthand.   There may be less rude comments which are useful for family history: 'he married the daughter of Mr Jones of Newton', 'the first that ever sowed sainfoin in these parts', or 'his family came out of Scottland'.

Some of the clergy were interested in medical matters, and give causes of death - almost always if there is an epidemic of plague or fever. Although it was mainly the country clergy who had the leisure to do this, the cause of death is recorded consistently for some years in busy town parishes like St Mary Whitechapel, and Sheffield. There are sad stories of whole families dying within a month of some contagion.

Strangers dying in a parish may have their place of origin given (probably in hope of recovering the cost of burial). If any of these are spotted, it is helpful to note them and send them to the Family History Society of the home area.

The printed registers of 1813 leave little space for comments and additional remarks, so that there was a loss of detail in a number of parishes.

From 1783 to 1794 you will notice in burial registers 'pd 3d' or 'P' against entries.   A tax of threepence was imposed on all entries registered, unless the person was too poor to pay. The clergy resented being used as unpaid tax collectors, so they tended to let anyone who did not appear on a tax-paying list off the payment and set them down as 'P' for pauper.   The note 'pd 3d' indicates that the person was well off, on uncommonly law-abiding.

The name of a person with property is often underlined and/or the word 'Mortuary' added.   This means that the clergyman had claimed from the executors the customary fee of ten shillings for an estate worth £40 or over, which had been a legal fee in Tudor times. Anyone labelled 'Mr' is a gentleman, a rich man, or one worthy of honour in the parish.   'Mrs' is similarly used to indicate social status, not necessarily for a married lady.   The infant children of the Squire are called 'Mr' and 'Mrs' from baptism.

There may also be a fee for 'breaking the ground', payable for the first of a family of incomers buried in the churchyard, after which subsequent members had the right to burial.   If a couple moved away temporarily but were still legally settled in the parish, they might send their babies back to be buried at 'home'.   There was an extra fee for the burial of a non-settled person, even if he wished to be buried in the parish because distant ancestors came from it.   Burial in the church itself cost even more, and is a distinct status symbol.

Old Style - New Style

Before 1752, the year began on March 25 in church registers, which is why a baby can be born in December and baptised in January the same year.   When you are copying entries from registers before this date, for dates between January 1 and March 24, get into the habit of writing down the 'old style' date **and** the new one.   If the register says '14 January 1714' then it is 1715 in modern terms.   But if you correct it then and there, some time later you may wonder if the date is new-style 1715, or really 1716.   So write down '14 Jan 1714/5', then you will know just what was intended.

This Calendar reform was decreed by the Pope in 1582, and you will find some clergy using 'new style' then, but they were soon brought to heel and reverted, though some mutinously described it as 'after the style of the church of England'.   In Scotland, 'new style' was adopted in 1600, which could be important if you are working near the border even in England.

Quakers, oddly, followed church usage in naming their months. They did not use pagan names, but began their year in March as 'first month', so that, for instance, 7th month exactly translates the Latin 'September', 10th month is December, and so on.

At the same time as this reform in 1752, the calendar was corrected by the removal of eleven days (3-14 September), for the world had 'run fast' by that amount over the centuries.   People with birthdays after 2 September sometimes adjusted the date, which is why printed biographies may not tally with birth/baptism dates you find in registers.

The loss of eleven days was adjusted for in leases, and families no doubt had their own arrangements about missing birthdays, but the eleven days can make a difference to fine calculations of age around this period.   You will occasionally find people referring to 'old Michaelmas' or 'old Christmas Day'.   The most enduring reminder is the start of the modern financial year on 5 April, eleven days after the old New Year's Day of 25 March.

Baptismal customs

Parish registers do not normally include birth as well as baptismal dates, but some clergy did choose to state them, consistently or for a few years.   Where they are given, it is possible to work out the local 'custom' for baptising. Country baptisms in general took place at three to four weeks, the latter being more common, though in some areas, a week or a fortnight seems to have been the rule laid down by some long forgotten cleric.   Severe winter weather or distance from the church could extend this.

Town baptisms, where the infant was much more at risk from infection and poor sanitary conditions, often took place within days of birth. Too often, they are followed by a burial entry within the week. The wealthier town families would sometimes send the mother to the country home for the birth.

The first child of a couple might be born at home with Mum, or be brought back to the mother's house for baptism.   Some couples who moved to town, and perhaps ceased to attend church, might have the babies baptised when they came home on a visit to the grandparents, which gives a useful link with a distant address, especially a London one.

If an infant was frail, the clergyman would be sent for to 'half-baptise' the child at home, followed by the formal Christening ceremony with godparents in the church later on.   These are entered as 'private baptism', 'at home' (or 'domi' in the Latin period) and the later church ceremony as 'received into church', or 'R.I.C.'. In dire emergency, the midwife could baptise the child - in which case, the only register entry is likely to be a burial soon after. If, against expectation, the baby survived, the register may record that the midwife gave the wrong name, even one of the wrong sex in rare cases, or, in the early days, played safe and named the child 'creature of God'. By the early 1800s, private baptism had a certain social cachet in some areas, and the gentry and rich farmers used to send for the parson as a matter of course rather than necessity.

Extra names can be added at baptism, or the original name altered. There is provision for baptismal names to be added to a birth certificate within a year of registration, though this is rarely formally done. Nowadays, we all know someone who has taken against the name they were originally given and is known for all purposes by a different one, which can cause problems of proving identity or tracing ancestry. It did happen occasionally in earlier centuries, but is difficult to prove, though well-documented cases of 'Mercy' and 'Honor' becoming Mary and Hannah, after breaking with the chapel, or baptised Edmunds becoming Edwards (and *vice versa*) are known. Ann and Agnes, Jane and Joan, Mary Ann and Marion, Betty and Elizabeth, are always recognised variants of the same name.

It is never safe to assume that a multiple baptism is one of twins, triplets ... sextuplets, unless it fills a regular two-year slot in the family. More often, it will be that of a family of nonconformists who have seen the light, willingly, or because they were forced to it to claim parish relief. Sometimes the clergyman will state the age of children above infancy, or even older than the norm of weeks for the parish. Nonconformist parents might bring a sickly baby to church, with a kind of superstitious feeling than conformity might save its life. For the poor, it might be a condition of receiving treatment from the doctor paid by the parish.

A marriage followed by a (perhaps rapid) first baptism, a second in about a year, and others at two or two-and-a-half year intervals, with the last child after a longer gap, extending over a period of twenty-odd years, is a 'complete' family. There are endless variations but a break in the pattern may mean a move to another nearby parish, or a period of local or personal malnutrition.

Infant mortality was very high, and it was customary to name a succession of sons with one name until one survived. Very occasionally, where a legacy hung on having a son named Thomas, and the current incumbent was sickly, a second baby might be given the name as well. In ordinary families, duplication rarely occurs at all, and then mainly in a second family, after the first family are married and away.

In the earlier registers, some babies who died were designated 'chrisomers'. In some places, this has the strict meaning of a baby baptised, and wrapped in a chrisom cloth, but dying before the mother was 'churched' at six weeks after the birth. In other places, it referred to any baby dying after birth but before baptism, still in swaddling bands and technically unnamed.

Double names are rare before 1660 and then occur at first mostly in gentry families. 'Posthumous' as a second name for a child born after the father's death is met. Courtiers added the monarch's name to their son's first name - with curious effect in the time of Queen Anne for William Anne Keppel. Double-naming slowly spread down the social scale, but at any time before 1800 in towns and 1830+ in the country it may indicate social status or ambition. The upper classes retaliated by giving triple or quadruple names as the custom spread. A surname used as second forename may imply hopes of inheritance from the person whose name is used, but far more often indicates illegitimacy.

Illegitimacy

There are a number of expressions found in parish registers denoting bastardy. These are fully listed in the *Illegitimacy* Guide in this series (page 32). They are normally obvious - base, spurious, 'son of the people' are common terms. In many of the older registers the father's name is stated too. If he is called 'reputed' it means that paternity was certainly known; if 'imputed' that he has been accused but it hadn't finally been settled (on the other hand, if the parson had had any doubt, he wouldn't have used the name). As mentioned (page 4), paternity could be shown when naming the child by using the father's name as well.

Burials in woollen; 'Collectioners'

In 1666 and again in 1678, the flagging wool trade was encouraged by a law that all corpses should be buried 'in sheep's wool only', on pain of a fine payable to the poor box. The gentry still used silk or linen shrouds, and it seemed to be a point of honour for all of them, magistrates as well, to break the law in this way, rather than 'cheat the poor men's box'.

The relatives or friends of every deceased person had to swear an oath before the local J.P. or a clergyman of another parish that the body had been 'buried in wollen' within eight days, and this may be written in a special book, or simply recorded in the ordinary burial register as 'affidavit', 'afadavy', or 'Aff.' against the name.

The word 'Collectioner' or 'Coll^r·' is sometimes added to names in the burials. This means that the deceased was in receipt of parish relief, collected from the better-off as poor rate.

Missing burials

Occasionally, there is no trace of the burial of an infant, though he is replaced by another of the same name. Possibly the little body was slipped in the coffin of a relative, to save a fee. Possibly the corpse was buried on land belonging to the family. Small bones were frequently discovered in fields in the last war, when new ground was broken for planting. A young wife dying in childbirth of her first infant is sometimes taken back home for burial with her own family. The death of paupers may be recorded in detail in the Overseers'

accounts.   Adults may die on a journey and money may not have been
available for them to be brought home.   Husbands sometimes vanished
from home (which may be commented on in the Overseers' accounts) and
it was accepted even by the clergy that a woman deserted, with no news
of her husband for seven years, might marry again. Rarely, the delin-
quent returns in old age to reclaim his home.

Nonconformists and clandestine marriages

Often, the only trace of a family is a marriage, followed by a
few burials, and then a new generation of marriages twenty-odd years
later. If you meet this, you may have nonconformists on your hands.
Sometimes the clergyman forced a baptism as a condition of marriage,
in which case it will be on the same day or very near the day of
marriage.

The really determined Dissenter might marry before his own folk at
the meeting, making a declaration of intent first. This was more or
less legal under common law, and certainly so if the pastor involved
had Anglican orders.   Quakers, Jews and Catholics married in their
own assemblies without a qualm. Ordinary Protestant Dissenters mixed
more with the general populace and were more vulnerable to moral
pressures.   If they owned any property, or their families did, they
would often feel it was safer to marry in a church. The local parish
church was out - it left them open to teasing, forced baptism and
other indignities.

Every county had churches and isolated (Anglican) chapels known as
'places of resort' where the clergyman would marry anyone to anyone
if they crossed his palm with silver. Often these were tiny parishes
with little income of their own.   In Buckinghamshire, a parish with
a total population of 20-25 had an average of 23 marriages a year,
and similar examples were found all over the country. Some of these
clergy seem to have laid in a job lot of licences, which they issued
at cut rates to all comers. There is a testy complaint that one un-
sporting groom had 'come with his own licence', thus cutting retail
profits. Londoners, even, came out to country parishes, and country-
men went up to town, to places like St James Dukes Place, where this
easy-going attitude prevailed, to the extent of 30 to 40 marriages a
day. Ecclesiastical sanctions were brought against some of the London
clergy who had most offended, which left the way clear for the non-
beneficed marriage mongers. The parish clergy could do little against
them, and even threats of imprisonment were to no avail, for most of
them were already prisoners.

Younger sons of gentry often took orders while they were at Univer-
sity without any intent to serve a benefice, with the idea that if a
fat family living became vacant when they were ready to settle down,
they would be qualified. Meanwhile, they pursued the common rackety
course of life of gentlemen of the time, and often ended up in debt,
and in a Debtors' Prison, of which the most famous was the Fleet in
Faringdon Street. Originally, marriage took place inside the prison,
and when this was stopped, the debtor-clergy obtained permission to

live just outside it, in the 'Rules or Liberties' of the Fleet. Here
the parsons would marry anyone for a fee, day or night, and they did
a roaring trade with sailors on shore, visitors to London, and couples
whose families opposed the match.   If the husband repented of the
bargain, they would tear the page out of their 'registers' for a further fee.   Several of the notebooks kept by these parsons have been
deposited at the Public Record Office and some years ago a transcription was started, which seems to have vanished. There are transcripts
of some of the minor churches which operated a marriage racket.

Some of the clergy made ample money to get them out of gaol, but
preferred to stay within the 'Rules' or opened Marriage shops, with
facilities for the ceremony and the wedding breakfast too, on the
fringes of London as it then was. So did innkeepers, spotting a pro-
fitable sideline, with ample clergy on tap.   A famous one was St
George's chapel, Mayfair, run by the Rev. Alexander Keith, whose
clientele was massive and varied. Because of later property develop-
ment, a marriage at 'St George's Mayfair' sounds classy, but at the
time it was a raffish area (as parts still are).

The marriages were legal (after some argument in court) but not
always stable, since many couples knew little about each other. Some
of the sailors came back with another bride next leave, and one lady
married two men in one day.   It was quick, cheerful and probably
filled a need for more than those for whom it dug a pit.

While it only involved members of the lower and lower middle
classes, no one much bothered, though the higher clergy denounced the
practice from time to time.   But the marriage shops would also cater
for the runaway heiress and her lover, asking no proof of age or consent of parents.   Once a girl was married to a fortune hunter, she
was ruined as currency on the marriage market.   The husband could
claim dowries and other sums left 'at her day of marriage' and use
them as he wished.   Even if she repented of the bargain, the husband
would still have the chance to run through her fortune, since divorce
was rare and cumbersome. It was this abuse, which affected the pock-
ets and pride of the legislating classes, which led to the passing of
the Hardwicke Act 'for the better prevention of Clandestine Marriage'
in 1753, whose effects have already been described.

How far back can I go?

Parish registers were first ordered to be kept in 1538, by Thomas
Cromwell, Henry VIII's Vicar General, after the Dissolution of the
Monasteries.   Before that, the monks had kept unsystematic notes of
births, marriages and deaths of noble and wealthy families as an aid
to proving age for inheritance purposes.   Cromwell ordered that *all*
people's events should be recorded, and it is naive to assume that
what he was after was not just easing succession of heirs or checking
cousin marriage, but establishing population statistics, for poll tax
purposes.

The clergy were perhaps the only local persons who could write,
and the Church had been established by the King, so it was the ideal

organisation to collect his required information. The clergy resented
this co-option into the 'civil service' unpaid, and the further away
from London they were, the less enthusiasm they tended to show for
beginning the task.

The law said that all baptisms, marriages and deaths were to be
written down in a book after service on Sunday evenings, in the presence of the churchwardens. In the country, these men were possibly
illiterate, and had their farm animals to see to, Sunday or not, so
the task tended to be put off till later. The fall of Cromwell in
1540 removed pressure from the centre, and in many places it was not
until reminders in 1558 that they got started at all. Some registers
appear to have been kept on loose paper sheets, and this caused con-
cern to the all-seeing eye of Elizabeth I.

In 1597, it was ordered that all existing registers were to be
copied into 'fair parchment books', at least from the beginning of
her own reign. In large parishes, this was a mammoth task. Wealthy
clergy coped by hiring a scrivener to do the work. The less affluent
might buckle to and do the job as intended, and some unwary searchers
have been known to swear that the same clergyman was in a certain
parish for sixty or more years, led astray by the same writing for
years in this copy register. Some clergy started their task at 1558,
ignoring what had gone before. Some started manfully, and then either
eased their task by cutting down the wording to the bare minimum, or
left out parts of years or even a stretch of ten or twenty years. If
the number of events per year drops suddenly from twenty to three, or
there is a gap, you can suspect the clergyman's energy, rather than
that all his parishioners suddenly stopped giving birth (or even
stopped dying). Rarely, the original paper register has survived and
comparison can be made, showing neglect.

What details are given?

There was no rule about the precise form the entries should take.
It was entirely up to the clergyman whether he chose to record:
        Baptysed John son of John Smithe
        Baptised John Smyth sunn of John Smith
        Baptised John ye sonne of Joh. and Marie Smytthe
        Baptised John Smith ye secant soone of John Smythe ye carpenter
            and of Marie his wyf
or just
        Baptised Joh. Smith.
The first form is by far the commonest, since mere mothers were not
important.

Marriages normally record only the names of the couple:
        John Smith married Mary Brown
but sometimes the event is entered merely as:
        John Smith married Mary
or even
        John Smith married his wyf.
Both baptismal and marriage entries tend to name mother or wife more
often as time goes on.

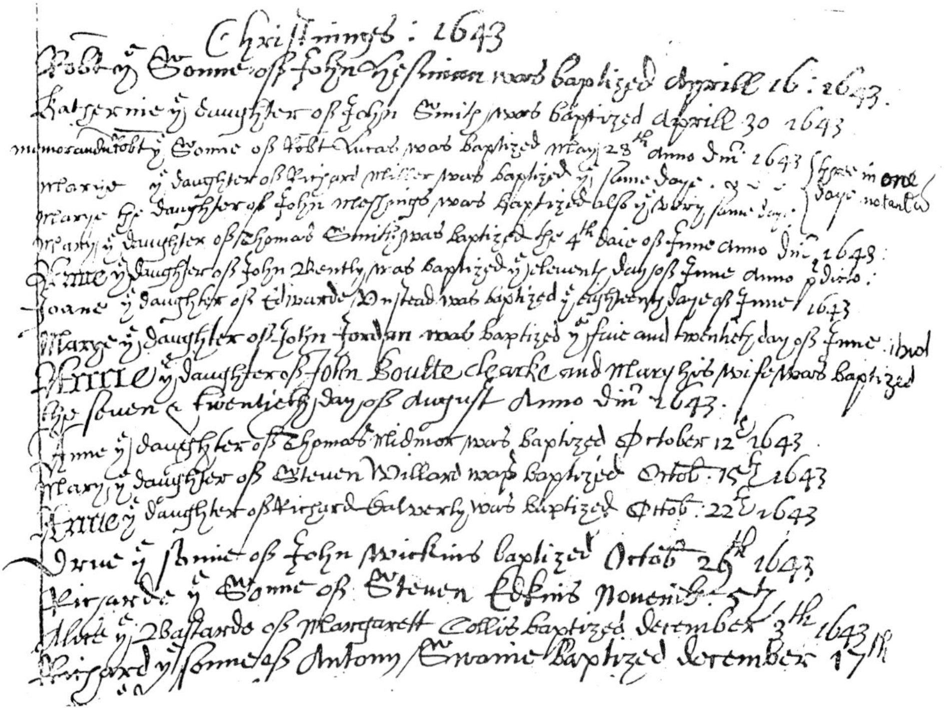

Christnings : 1643
Robert ye Sonne of John Chessman was baptized Aprill 16 : 1643.
Katherine ye daughter of John Smith was baptized Aprill 30 1643
memorandum Robert ye Sonne of Robt Curab was baptized May 28th Anno Dni 1643
Marye ye daughter of Richard Miller was baptized ye same daye.
Marye the daughter of John Massinge was baptized also ye very same day. these in one daye [illegible]
Martha ye daughter of Thomas Smith was baptized the 4th daie of June Anno Dni 1643
Anne ye daughter of John Bentley was baptized ye eleaventh day of June Anno pdicto.
Joane ye daughter of Edwarde Unstead was baptized ye eighteenth daye of June 1643
Marye ye daughter of John Jordan was baptized ye five and twentieth day of June ibid
Anne ye daughter of John Boutte clearke and Mary his wife was baptized the seven & twentieth day of August Anno Dni 1643.
Anne ye daughter of Thomas Widmer was baptized October 12th 1643
Mary ye daughter of Steven Willard was baptized Octob. 15th 1643
Anne ye daughter of Richard Calverly was baptized Octob. 22th 1643
Jane ye sonne of John Wickins baptized Octob 26th 1643
Richarde ye sonne of Steven Edkins Novemb. 5th
Alice ye Bastarde of Margarett Collis baptized December 3th 1643
Richard ye sonne of Antony Swaine baptized December 17th

Well-maintained **seventeenth century registers** *at Chiddingly, Sussex.*

Above: Baptisms, with prominence from larger lettering for those considered important, such as the parson's own daughter Anne. Below: Burials, with that of a centenarian and other supplementary information.

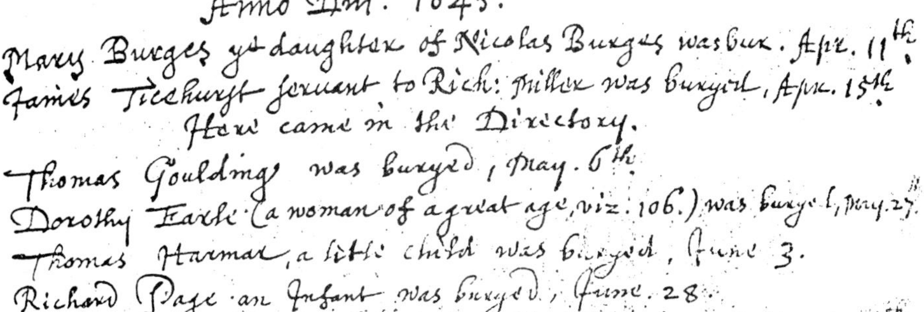

Anno Dni. 1645.
Mary Burges ye daughter of Nicolas Burges was bur. Apr. 11th.
James Ticehurst servant to Rich: Miller was buryed, Apr. 15th.
Here came in the Directory.
Thomas Goulding was buryed, May. 6th.
Dorothy Earle (a woman of a great age, viz: 106.) was buryed, May. 27th.
Thomas Harman, a litle child was buryed, June 3.
Richard Page an Infant was buryed, June. 28.
Joane Sims ye wife of Thomas Sims was buryed, Aug. 12th.
Edward Quickhampton, a litle child was buryed, Sept. 10th.
Catherine a base borne child of Phineas Payne was buryed, Sept. 19th.

Burial entries may give the name only, but often extra information
is added. Children may be labelled with their father's name and wives
with their husband's - though sometimes the entry is for:

ye wyf of John Smith

without further name stated.   If other entries read this way, then
probably a male name without further description is an adult.   If
anyone attained a great age (over 75 was antique) this may be stated:

Buried John Brown, of the age of 90 yeres as he sayth.

Deaths of the gentry or the clergyman's own kin are sometimes writ
large, followed by a eulogy, in English or Latin.   But less exalted
persons may have their own memorial:

Buryed Solomon Sotherden an honest miller: there be not many such

Rychard Snatchell, a stout young man, a curious blacksmith died
    of ye smallpoxe and was buried the last day of Maye [1643]

Buried Mary West strumpet to John Harris.

As mentioned above (page 10), early registers sometimes have
entries mixed together, sometimes written up at the end of the year
with baptisms, etc., grouped together, sometimes with baptisms, marriages and burials in separate sections of pages - always check.

Clerk's rough books

Sorting of the registers was made possible because the parish clerk
kept a rough Day Book in which events were entered as they occurred.
These were then copied out into the 'fair register' by the clerk himself or the parson, at intervals, and, in small parishes, sometimes
only at the end of the year, as above.   If the clerk wrote badly,
scribbled entries on loose sheets of paper, or lost his book during
the year, there were errors or omissions in the final record.   Where
rough books survive (as in Banbury, Oxfordshire) it is possible to
spot these, but most books probably were kept in the clerk's hands
and possibly destroyed when they were full.   Even where they do survive and give an obviously more accurate statement of affairs, they
are not legal evidence, any more than are Bishop's Transcripts (see
page 23).

In town parishes, the clerk was a full-time and important official.
Originally, he would have been in minor orders and have played a great
part in the service, reading lessons and singing masses, acting as
choir master and schoolmaster too. The clerical functions were whitt-
led down, but the clerk carried out the functions of a secretary,
accounts clerk, straight man and bouncer; he kept the rough registers
and usually made the fair copies; collected fees, wrote lists of banns
for the parson to read out, staved off importunate parishioners and
arranged 'house calls' to the sick and dying; he led the hymns and
psalms and intoned responses in church, noted absentees from services,
accompanied the minister on official business and so on.

The country parish did not provide enough trade for a full-time
clerk, so generally the job was doubled by the schoolmaster (if there
was one) or a local shoemaker or tailor who happened to be able to
read and write, if he was not hurried.   In this case, a good singing

voice was probably the main consideration.   Country clerks may have
a good, round handwriting, but spelling that is gallant rather than
accurate ('Meary', 'Tommus', 'Pernalerpay'); some write with hands
more accustomed to the bradawl, or as with a pitchfork dipped in
manure.   But if the clergyman himself takes on the task of writing
the 'fair copy', you may be faced with educated but crabbed ortho-
graphy, and aggressive use of Latin (see page 25).

Errors in the registers

Where a clergyman copies from a clerk's book, or even where the
clerk himself copies from inadequate notes, mistakes can arise.   If
the name of a mother is not entered at the time, it may be wrongly
given in a baptism – it was not regarded of primary importance.
Frequently, the name of the child is repeated as that of the mother –
sometimes the father's name is incorrect in this way.   If you have a
run of baptisms to Thomas and Kezia, interspersed with one for 'Mary
daughter of Thomas and Mary', or 'John son of John and Kezia', it is
probably a clerical error. 'Jno' (John) may be read as 'Tho' (Thomas)
and *vice versa*, 'Marg' for Margaret read as 'Mary', 'hanah' as Sarah
and so on.

Mere 'spelling mistakes' should be expected. There was no standard
spelling of names before 1870, when Board Schools attempted to impose
it.   If a name sounds right, it is right.   You will soon forget that
'we always spell it with an H' (if you are wise), when you find:

May 6   baptised John Osborn sun to John Osbourne

May 8   buried the said John Usband sonne to Husband the miller.
Usborne, Horborne, Asburn are other standard variants of that name.

Uncommon names not familiar to the clergyman may be 'translated'
into common ones and only a literate and determined man could get
this altered later.

The Commonwealth registers

The style of entry was at the discretion of the local clergyman,
and in the mid-seventeenth century, some had grown very slack.   They
also included many Royalists, totally opposed to the deposition and
beheading of Charles I in 1649, and most of these were ejected in
favour of good Puritans, some of whom were better ideologists and
preachers than penmen.   To remedy the poor register keeping, Oliver
Cromwell (2Xgt grand-nephew of Thomas) decreed that from 1653, all
register-keeping should be taken out of the hands of the clergy and
transferred to a layman called the 'Parish Register', chosen from
among the locals and ratified by a magistrate.   Some of the men
selected were excellent record keepers, some were no doubt good Party
men, but dreadful writers and spellers.   In some villages, the only
man who could write well enough was the old parish clerk, or even the
parson.

In 1653, all birth and death dates were to be recorded in a book
set aside for this.   Sometimes the Register got possession of the
church books, sometimes they were withheld. Some baptismal dates were

given as well or the system reverted to the old form after a year or three.

Marriages were no longer to take place in church. Intention to marry was to be proclaimed three times in the Market Place or, failing this, from the Church porch, and the couple were then to go before a Justice of the Peace to be legally joined. Not all J.Ps. cooperated enthusiastically, with the result that parishes adjacent to a marrying justice may contain the proclamations of people from a distance away, and other places have almost no marriage records at all. Many of the locals felt that the new system was not a proper marriage, and slipped off to church as well, where clergy who had managed to stay in office wed them secretly.

In a properly kept Commonwealth register, the name, occupation, parish and father's name of the groom and the name, parish and father's name of the bride should be given - details only carried on in Quaker registers thereafter. Market towns often have the best collection of marriages from far and wide.

After Cromwell died and the King was restored in 1660, the Registers were dismissed (unless they were the parish clerks, who simply adapted the form of entry). Restored Royalist clergy often seized the books and destroyed them, then found that they had wiped out seven years of the history of the parish. The conscientious ones therefore went round local families, collecting entries from family Bibles, or dates of birth of children roughly remembered. This will not cover the folk who found it prudent to move house, to avoid retribution from those to whom they were known as 'Oliver's men'.

Puritanism did not die with Oliver, and in many parishes, the register entries of the 1660s by no means cover all the people living in the parish, as found in other sources.

Just after 1660, there was a great drive by the Bishops to locate and punish any lurking Puritans and the results of this 'search and destroy' mission may be found among the Bishops' Registers. Each parish was to 'present' or accuse any persons living there who were not married (in church) or who failed to attend Sunday worship there. Many who had legally married before Justices had to remarry in church or have their children branded bastards by a hard-line local parson.

Although Commonwealth marriages before Justices were legalised after the Restoration, many local clergy did not accept this and labelled the offspring sneeringly as 'Smith alias Jones'. Marriages by sectarian lay preachers were never fully legalised, though good under common law, and although some couples persisted in following the same system after 1660. This didn't matter a lot unless the father had property, in which case he might marry formally to keep it in the family. The Bishop's Registers may list a couple and their teenage children as non-churchgoers, which helps to cover events otherwise now missing, in what is known as 'the Commonwealth gap'.

Punitive laws and heavy fines forced many families of 'Dissenters' to attend church from time to time, when the heat was on, and this 'occasional conformity' and group baptisms, especially when the father of a family died, may be the only evidence that they are there. There were still enough Dissenters around for the law to require the listing of their births, as well as baptisms of the conformers. Incentive was provided in form of a sixpenny fee to the parson from the parents. Often the Dissenters' births are listed at the end of a year, or separately in the register, and awkward clergy will only state 'a son of James Brown was born', not give him the name used by the family, since he had not been baptised in church.

Sometimes age and poverty forced a long-term Dissenter to get baptised. The oldest persons I have myself found were a pair of sisters, 72 and 74, both widowed and in need of parish relief, in 1742. 'Adult' baptisms (anything over about 14) do not always have the names of parents, unfortunately.

Vindictiveness may be carried to the grave. Few nonconformists had access to alternative burial grounds, so they ended in the church-yard:

    Hurled into the ground at night with no service.

Even their names were challenged:

    Buryed a person known by the name of Mary Fenn an Anabaptist.

She had been known by that name for upwards of 65 years and might have been allowed it in death.

Bishops' Transcripts

Mention has been made several times of Bishops' Transcripts (BTs). Irregularly from 1561 in some dioceses and for every year from 1598, the clergyman was ordered to send in an exact copy of registers to the Bishop. In practice, the collection was deputed to his Archdeacon, who was supposed to travel round each parish every Easter. This wasn't practical either, so generally the Archdeacon went to one of a group of parishes and the neighbouring clergy brought in their copies. You may see a note in the register that all names to a certain date were 'handed in at ye Visitation'.

By no means all the runs of BTs are complete. Some of the clergy failed to turn up, and the Archdeacon had to remember to chase them up next year, or to send his Apparitor (a sort of trouble-shooter) to collect. Some of the copies were made on small scraps of paper or parchment (it cost money) cut from the spaces on other parish docu-ments, or old records no longer current. These small scraps got lost easily or might be used for stiffening the backs of limp books.

The BT may be less full than the original parish register entry. Sometimes, illegitimate children were not included in the BT, and personal comments about parishioners are normally omitted, since they would mean nothing to the Archdeacon. However, occasionally the BT was copied up directly from the Clerk's rough book by a clergyman who then failed to make the same entries in the parish registers, so there is sometimes fuller information in the BT. Sometimes, where the registers are damaged or damp-stained, the BT is much more legible, and it always pays to compare the two entries where they are both available.

The making of copies for the Bishop was declared illegal from 1641 and effectively ceased in 1645 (when Bishops were abloished) for all good Commonwealth men.   However, with the perverse quality which is typically English, some of the clergy who hadn't cared much in the past now copied out their registers diligently and used all kinds of subterfuges to get them to the Bishop or Archdeacon, risking punish-ment if they were found out.   Some of the restored clerics also solemnly copies out the old registers and sent the result in in 1661, as a gesture, but it is pretty rare to find such alternative records for the whole 'Commonwealth gap' period.

The survival of BTs varies widely from diocese to diocese, though presumably they were compiled everywhere at the time.   In some they may be found from the earliest years, the late sixteenth century and the reigns of James I and Charles I to 1642 (e.g. most of the Lincoln diocese); in others they may survive only from the late seventeenth century (Oxford, Hereford); some were burnt (Dorset before 1724), some reputed to have been evicted to make room for wine in the cellars (Wells pre-1750, Winchester pre-1780).   There are hardly any for the Diocese of London before 1800 - and that includes Middlesex, Essex and part of Hertfordshire.   Some have been damaged by poor storage over the centuries.

Those that survive are now mostly in the appropriate County Record Offices, though some have been committed to the charge of other institutions.   They are diocesan-based, which means, for instance, that those for Derbyshire, Staffordshire, part of Shropshire and Warwickshire are at Lichfield, in which diocese they were.

Details of those that survive, with some indiaction of their coverage, are given in the FFHS Guide to *Bishops' Transcripts and Marriage Licences: Their location and indexes* (see page 32).

Late starters and early finishers

Not all parishes existed in 1538.   Many places we think of as ancient towns were once mere hamlets in another parish, and shifts of population due to industry or landscape changes were at last recog-nised by the building of a 'chapel of ease' (daughter church) and then the formation of a new parish.   Liverpool was part of Walton on the Hill until the time of William III.   Macclesfield and Congleton were chapelries of the villages of Prestbury and Astbury until the mid-1700s.

London was forever developing. The Great Fire of 1666 burnt 84 of the 109 churches and many houses in the City, and this resulted in the combination of the existing parishes and the movement of residents out to Westminster and rural Marylebone or the fields of Stepney, with constant augmentation from outside.   Many new churches were built in the 1720s, including the fashionable St George's Hanover Square, and others were vastly expanded then and in the 1740s.   A new wave of building followed the influx of people in the 1830s and 40s, but in this century, many churches have become redundant.

A similar pattern on a smaller scale can be observed in any of the great industrial cities in the north. At any time, a move to the next street may change the parish completely and even people who stayed in the same place might find themselves in a different parish.

Once you have established a county of origin, it is useful to get a map showing the parishes (see page 32) which gives starting dates of registers. London is best covered by the Guides to parish registers prepared by Norman Graham (see page 32).

Latin in parish registers

In early registers, you will often come across Latin of a simple sort, used occasionally up to 1733 (when it ceased to be the legal language) and even after. It was the exception rather than the rule, but some clergymen were Classics scholars and preferred Latin, some had Latin thrust upon them, because the last man used it, and they didn't want to seem inferior. In this case, the grammar is sometimes suspect and 'Latin' words are formed by tacking 'us' on the end of a word for which there is a perfectly good Latin equivalent (like 'Williamus' instead of 'Gulielmus' for William).

A complete list of names, occupations, relationships, dates and phrases commonly found in parish registers is given in *Simple Latin* by Eve McLaughlin (90p including postage direct from the author). The absolutely basic terms are:

    filius = son of
    filia = daughter of (often abbreviated to 'fil.' or even 'fill.'
             by clerks who aren't Latin scholars)
    uxor   = wife of
    vidua = widow of
    senex = an old man
    generosus, armiger, miles = gent., arms-bearer, knight.

Male names generally end in '-us' or '-is'; female names end in '-a'. The three basic events are expressed:

    baptised = baptizat, baptizatus est, renatus (reborn)
    married = nupsit, matrimonium solemnizat, copulati or coniunc-
               tierant
    buried   = sepultat, sepultatus erat, in tumulo sep.

In some cases, personal comments on the character and habits of the dead are included. Eulogies were written in Latin, so were less favourable comments. Ask an archivist to help you, or copy exactly and consult an elderly teacher.

Reading the registers

If you are fortunate, there may be a transcription of the parish register you want to consult (always try to locate one before resorting to the original or its microfilm). But you have been warned even so not to accept it as the last word, and at some stage you will want to check it with the original register or BT, which may be presented on microfilms, not always very good quality.

In the nineteenth century, a clerk's handwriting will be very much like modern writing (though spelling may be odd), but some curates

seemed to grudge the ink expended, and the letters are pinched up,
with 'e' looking like 'i'. Always start there, to get familiar with
the surnames and local places mentioned.

In the eighteenth century, you will meet the 'long s' which looks
like an 'f' (and this hangs on into the 1800s too) and an 'e' which
looks like an 'o' with a curl in the top.

Before this, 'secretary hand' was used, in which some of the letters
look odd, especially the capitals. If you look at letters in familiar
Christian names and places, you should be able to read the surnames,
with a little practice. Other letters are differently written - 'c'
looks like 'r', and 'r' like 'u' or 'x'.

It is useful to arm yourself with a guide like *Reading Old Handwriting* by Eve McLaughlin (direct from the author, £1 including post)
giving examples of alphabets from 1600, 1700 and 1800, and there are
other similar guides.

Remember that you do not have to read every word on every page -
you will soon learn to recognise your own ancestral name.

Where are they now?

In an effort to safeguard registers from the depredations of the
elements, careless handling, vandalism and theft, there has been
encouragement for many years to deposit them in the Record Office of
the county concerned. This was given a boost in 1978 by the passing
of the Parochial Registers and Records Measure, which decreed that
all such records over 100 years old should be handed in, unless express
permission was obtained and very stringent storage and security re-
quirements met. To comply with these would cost the Parochial Church
Council a lot of money, so in most cases the measure has had the
desired effect. For further security of the originals, most record
offices have microfilmed the registers, and it is in this form that
they are presented to the searcher.

So the County Record Office is the first place to enquire about
the location and availability of registers. Some places also have
Area record offices or even town offices, and the best place to find
out about the existence, addresses and map location of these is in
the FFHS Guide to *Record Offices: Where to Find Them* (see page 32).
Most County Record Offices have some kind of list of what they hold
and there are more detailed Guides available for some places. There
is a fairly comprehensive list of registers deposited, countrywide,
published as *Original Parish Registers in R.Os. and Libraries* in five
booklets (see page 32).

London, an exceptionally complicated area, is covered by Norman
Graham's various guides. *London Local Archives: A Directory of Local
Authority R.Os. and Libraries*, is another useful work (see page 32).

The parishes were given five years to hand in their registers or
to go through the legal process for retaining them. There are still
a small number of clergy who have done neither and although a few are
genuine historical scholars with a real interest in their registers
and people, more may be plain awkward, or wish to retain the income
from fees.

Fees for inspection and undeposited registers

Most County Record Offices are free - Gloucester, Exeter, Plymouth
and the Diocesan Record Office at Canterbury charge for all access
and a few others charge small sums for use of some microfilms.

If the registers are still in the parish, there is a scale fee
based on the time taken for the search. This should not be more than
£3.50 for the first hour and £2.50 for any subsequent hour. However,
because of a badly worded leaflet sent round, some clergy are under
the impression that they need not allow 'general searches', but only
'particular searches' for a single event. This is illegal, but per-
suading them may be tough. In fact, you are allowed access 'at any
reasonable time', though an appointment should always be made.

If you find a register is in the parish, go to the CRO and use the
BTs first (see page 23), if these survive for the parish. This will
limit the time you need to spend in the church or parsonage. If
access is refused, consult the County Archivist, who may be able to
help, failing whom, contact the Rural Dean, the Archdeacon and the
Bishop, in that order.

It is the 'droppers in' who arrive on a clergyman's doorstep without
any warning, demanding to look at his registers there and then, who
sour his attitude to others. Most parish clergy are busy men, with
several churches to look after, and the registers may not even be in
his own hands, but those of a churchwarden (not legal, but if often
happens). There have in the past been careless or unscrupulous genealogists who have mishandled registers or even snipped bits out, which
is why access must be monitored now. It is a powerful argument for
sending all registers to County Record Offices, where they will be
properly cared for.

If you write asking a clergyman to search for you, then you must
expect to pay for his time. He may not be capable or or willing to do
the work and depute it to a churchwarden who is minimally interested.
Too many people have been told in the past that there was 'no trace'
of an entry, only to find it, where expected, years later, after
searching fruitlessly elsewhere. Unless you are fortunate enough to
find a local person who is able to read the registers and is know-
ledgeable about the parish history, then it is best to do the search
yourself or engage a professional to do it.

Transcribed and printed copies

Many registers were transcribed and printed at the end of the last
century or beginning of this, often at the expense of the local
gentry whose family figures in them, or by Societies with similar
financial backing. After conventional printing became too expensive,
there was a lull, but more recently, Family History Societies have
taken up the torch and publish in less fancy fashion. Many more
registers have been transcribed, typed and indexed, so that between
five and ten copies may exist. If you can locate them, it will save
you a lot of time.

In general, one copy will be in the parish and one in the local CRO and any Local Studies Library in the county. Another will probably be at the library of the Society of Genealogists, 14 Charterhouse Buildings, Goswell Road, London EC1M 7BA (tel. 01-251 8799). This may be used by non-members on payment of an hourly or daily fee, open Tuesday to Saturday. Sometimes another copy will be at the Guildhall Library, Aldermanbury, EC2P 2EJ (tel. 01-606 3030) (Monday - Saturday, no fee). Published lists of transcripts in the Society's library and elsewhere (much less complete) are available (see page 32).

It may be possible to borrow registers which are printed through your own public library (in the U.K.) if you locate the title in a book catalogue. Typescript copies must generally be consulted where they are deposited. Some are indexed (though not all indexes are perfect), some are not. For instance, the Phillimore series of marriages, transcribed and published in groups, county by county, have no indexes in the printed volumes - but they can be read much faster than can the originals (and most of them are included in more general indexes, see pages 29-30).

Transcripts are only as good as the person who made them - which is sometimes not very good at all, since the transcribers sometimes were not expert palaeographers, but were too pigheaded to ask for help. Even the Phillimore series had errors and omissions enough to make a genealogist weep. However, anything is better than nothing and if you find a large deposit of 'yours' in a parish, but the direct ancestor does not figure in the index, it is wise to study the whole volume - it could be a poor indexer, it could be bad reading. Eventually, you will want to check the transcript against the original register anyway.

If you locate the parish in which your ancestors lived, and there is a printed copy of the register available for sale, do buy it - not just extract the names. Your money will help to pay the printing bill and may encourage that society to produce more, which could have other people's ancestors, or even more of your own. Besides, it is fun to flip a book open and say, 'this is my great-great-grandfather's baptism'.

Which parish? Indexes and finding aids

Sometimes you know which county your ancestors came from, but not where. Sometimes the parish in which you have located them 'runs dry'. Where can you go now?

If they were comfortably off, the wills for the county or even Prerogative Court wills should help. If they were really poor, then a systematic study of settlement papers should produce something. These two sources are discussed in detail in *Wills before 1858* and *Annals of the Poor* in this series (see page 32 and back cover).

There are also general collections of name references which may help. Most counties have some sort of 'Name Index' in the CRO where references to a particular surname are collected. The best of its

kind is the Essex CRO index, from which is is easy to trace movements
in the county. Such indexes are listed in the FFHS guide *Unpublished
Personal Name Indexes in Record Offices and Libraries* (see page 32).

The International Genealogical Index

The Mormon International Genealogical Index (I.G.I.) is a compila-
tion of baptisms, births and marriages, drawn either from microfilms
of whole registers for a certain period, or from names collected by
individual church members researching their own ancestors. The entries
have been fed into a computer and indexed on microfiches, county by
county for England, in a single sequence for Ireland and Scotland
(1981, now by county) and surname and Christian name sequences for
Wales and Monmouth (other countries of the world are also covered).
Burials are not included, though some 'deaths as infant' are indicated,
but not consistently.

Complete copies of this are held by the Society of Genealogists;
by main Mormon Stake Libraries; and by certain Family History Societies.
There are partial copies in CROs and Libraries all round the country.
Holdings of the 1981 edition in the U.K. are listed in the FFHS guide
Where to Find the I.G.I. (see page 32). The 1984 edition is becoming
generally available during 1986.

Not every entry in this index is accurate - the skill of the person
supplying the information is the governing factor. However, it is
possible to search a whole county, or the whole country, to locate
large deposits of the surname concerned, and possibly even the exact
entry, though this is in stylised form, and will have to be checked
with the originals later. Coverage of parishes varies greatly from
county to county - much depends on earlier transcription or the Mor-
mons' microfilming programme - but it is a very useful finding aid
and guide to the area where there are a lot of ancestral voices.

Marriage indexes

Most counties now have at least one Marriage Index, run by the
Family History Society or individuals. Most are still in progress,
but some cover the whole county, possibly for a period shorter than
1538-1837, which everyone aims at. Some started with blanket coverage
for 1813-37, for instance. They are listed in the FFHS guide to
Marriage, Census and Other Indexes (see page 32). This gives the
address to write to and fees for consultation. The fees are not
generally returnable if your particular marriage is not there - you
pay for the search of hundreds of parishes at a swoop, which could
otherwise take you years. Some Indexers will hold your request and
send you the details if the marriage comes in later, which is useful.
Even if it takes place outside the county, news may eventually filter
back, and then to you.

Most indexes give the full entry as it appears in the registers,
others the year date only, which means you have to check it later.
Some indexes do not list the brides under their own name, which is a
pity, since the females are the ones who tend to marry in the 'home'

parish. If the index is not phonetic, you will have to list all the variant spellings yourself, when you ask.

Boyd's Marriage Index

This is an earlier attempt at a national Marriage Index, compiled by counties, though some (and some periods) are much better covered than others. It is arranged mainly by county, in quarter centuries, sometimes with separate sequences for males and females, with variant spellings of surnames grouped together under one version (which is sometimes a bit odd, though cross-references are given). The marriages were mostly drawn from printed (such as the Phillimore series) or typescript transcripts of registers, with some from private manuscript ones, and as it was compiled some time ago, the access was not so easy or full as now.

There is a complete copy at the Society of Genealogists and partial copies elsewhere in the counties concerned. The parishes and periods included are listed in the Society's guide (see page 32).

Pallot Index

This Index (privately owned by the Institute of Heraldic and Genealogical Studies, Northgate, Canterbury, Kent CT1 1BA) is particularly strong on the London area, 1800-1837, but includes some entries from most counties. A basic guide to the parishes covered is available at £1 from the Institute. Coverage of this, also of Boyd, is given in *The Phillimore Atlas and Index of Parish Registers* (see p.32). This also includes a list of Marriage Indexes and an indication of which parishes may be included (as at 1984). For up-to-date information on location and conditions/fees for search in such indexes (and latest coverage) the FFHS Guide *Marriage, Census and other Indexes* (which is regularly updated) should be consulted, as indexers and their addresses change constantly. Invariably when enquiring a stamped, addressed envelope and initial contribution of £1.00 should be sent, unless it is known a larger sum is required.

Check your references

Although a search of any printed source or any index may set you on the right track again if you are floundering, it is never safe to assume that the man you lost in Devon is the one who turns up in Yorkshire, especially if the surname is common. Sooner or later, you will have to check every detail you have obtained from a secondary source with the original to make sure it is accurate, and also have to prove without doubt the connection. A pedigree based solely on the I.G.I. will not do - there are no burials (though certain child deaths are indicated) and too often the great-grandfather lovingly selected turns out to have died in his teens. However, what you find will, if it shows a deposit of the family name, probably lead to the right place, and work done on the wider family is never wasted.

Scottish registers

All Scottish 'old parish registers' (OPRs) were called in to Edinburgh in 1855, when registration there began.   They are now kept at the General Register Office, New Register House, West Register Street, Edinburgh EH1 3YT (tel. 031-556 3952)(this is off Princes Street, opposite the North British Hotel). There is a fee for access of £3.50 a day, with lower daily cost for longer periods.

Such registers rarely survive for country parishes before 1700 or even later, reflecting the later arrival of strong central administration than in the south.   There are good runs for Edinburgh and Glasgow parishes and some others before this.

In baptisms, almost all registers consistently show the full name of the mother with her maiden surname, which is useful in distinguishing families in a country with a number of persons of the same surname and Christian name in the same place. They are generally quite outspoken about whether the child is lawful, or begotten in fornication or adultery.   The accompanying Kirk Sessions records, which should always be consulted, state also which children arrived within eight months of marriage and record penances for bastardy and fornication.

Marriages tend to be noted as 'intent to marry' (like the Commonwealth Proclamations, see page 22) and the actual date of the ceremony may not be given. Frequently, there are no burials at all until the mid-nineteenth century.   Deaths can be traced in the Kirk Sessions records by a fee for 'hire of the mortcloth' (a pall for the coffin).

All OPRs are steadily being transcribed, surname indexed and put on microfiche, and sets are being sold to reference libraries in the counties of Scotland and to other organisations, so that access will eventually be possible in a variety of places apart from Edinburgh. There is also an index only to some OPRs and to events after 1855 in the I.G.I. (see page 29).

Irish registers – Church of Ireland

In 1864 Irish (Protestant) parish registers were similarly ordered to be sent in to the Irish Record Office in Dublin. Those which had been deposited were mainly destroyed when the Four Courts buildings were burnt in 1922.   Despite this catastrophe, a surprising amount of the information they contained has survived in transcript, or in originals which for some reason were not there at the time.   See Michael Leader's contribution 'Church Registers in Ireland' in the first *Family History Annual*, 1986 (page 32), and for detailed information consult the Irish Record Office or the Northern Ireland Record Office as appropriate.

Enquiries may also be made in the parishes, but do not expect a rapid answer or any. Northern Irish parishes are more likely to survive locally. Many Presbyterian registers are available at the Presbyterian Historical Society Library.

Catholicism was technically illegal before 1830, but flourishing, A good many registers survive in fact from the eighteenth century (and as they were not called in to the Record Office, escaped destruction), though they are generally of baptisms and perhaps marriages, but rarely burials.   Many of these registers are still with the priest.   Film copies of many have been deposited in Dublin at the Record Office, but permission from the priest may be required unless the Bishop has given blanket permission for personal research.

Of the relatively few records which survive, a proportion will be found in the I.G.I. for Ireland (see page 29).

BIBLIOGRAPHY

In addition to the titles below, all mentioned in the text, the Society of Genealogists' series *The National Index of Parish Registers* is recommended.   Three introductory volumes, and a separate Scottish volume, all by D.J. Steel, cover the subject of parish and non-parochial registers exhaustively and authoritatively. Other regional volumes give listings of parishes, details of registers and transcripts, and of non-parochial registers.

Federation of Family History Societies publications are obtainable from the FFHS, 17 Foxlea Road, Hailey Green, Halesowen B63 1DX. Society of Genealogists publications are obtainable from the Society, 14 Charterhouse Buildings, Goswell Road, London EC1M 7BA.

Page

8,24   *Bishops' Transcripts and Marriage Licences: A Guide to their Location and Indexes*. J.S.W. Gibson. FFHS, 2nd edition, 1986. £1.00 + 20p p&p.

  8   *My Ancestor was Jewish: How can I find out more about him?* Ed. Michael Gandy. Society of Genealogists, 1982. £1.80 + 35p p&p.

  9   *My Ancestors were Quakers: How can I find out more about them?* Edward H. Milligan and Malcolm J. Thomas. Soc. of Genealogists, 1983. £2.00 + 35p p&p.

 15   *Illegitimacy*. Eve McLaughlin. FFHS, 1986. 75p + 25p p&p.

 25   Individual County Parish Maps, England, Wales, Scotland.   The Institute of Heraldic & Genealogical Studies, 79-82 Northgate, Canterbury, Kent CT1 1BA. £2.20 incl. postage. Note: These maps are also published in *The Phillimore Atlas*, see right.

25,26 *The Genealogist's Consolidated Guide to Parish Register Copies and Indexes in the Inner London area: 1538-1837*; the same for the *Outer London area*; and for *Inner London Nonconformist Registers*. All compiled and arranged by Norman H. Graham, £2-3.00, from the author, 69 Crest View Drive, Petts Wood, Kent BR5 1BX.

 25   *Simple Latin*. Eve McLaughlin. 90p incl. postage from the author, Varneys, Rudds Lane, Haddenham, Bucks.

 26   *Reading Old Handwriting*. Eve McLaughlin. £1.00 from the author.

 26   *Record Offices: How to Find Them*. Jeremy Gibson and Pamela Peskett. FFHS, 3rd edition, 1986.   £1.50 + 20p p&p.